DEADLY DROUGHTS

By Michael Rajczak

Gareth Stevens
PUBLISHING

Please visit our website, www.garethstevens.com. For a free color catalog of all our high-quality books, call toll free 1-800-542-2595 or fax 1-877-542-2596.

Cataloging-in-Publication Data

Names: Rajczak, Michael.
Title: Deadly droughts / Michael Rajczak.
Description: New York : Gareth Stevens Publishing, 2017. | Series: Where's the water? | Includes index.
Identifiers: ISBN 9781482446807 (pbk.) | ISBN 9781482446821 (library bound) | ISBN 9781482446814 (6 pack)
Subjects: LCSH: Droughts–Juvenile literature.
Classification: LCC QC929.24 R36 2017| DDC 551.57′73–dc23

First Edition

Published in 2017 by
Gareth Stevens Publishing
111 East 14th Street, Suite 349
New York, NY 10003

Copyright © 2017 Gareth Stevens Publishing

Designer: Katelyn E. Reynolds
Editor: Kristen Nelson

Photo credits: Cover, p. 1 Sunny Forest/Shutterstock.com; cover, pp. 1–24 (background) vitalez/Shutterstock.com; pp. 4–21 (circle splash) StudioSmart/Shutterstock.com; p. 5 Becky Wass/Shutterstock.com; p. 7 Mark Wilson/Getty Images; p. 8 Tim Roberts Photography/Shutterstock.com; p. 9 Angel DiBilio/Shutterstock.com; p. 11 Paisarn Praha/Shutterstock.com; p. 13 (inset) Drozhzhina Elena/Shutterstock.com; p. 13 (main) Chr. Schipflinger/Moment/Getty Images; p. 15 Songquan Deng/Shutterstock.com; p. 17 (inset) PhotoQuest/Getty Images; p. 17 (main) Daniel J Bryant/Moment/Getty Images; p. 19 Rob Lind/EyeEm/Getty Images; p. 21 T.Dallas/Shutterstock.com.

Printed in the United States of America

CPSIA compliance information: Batch #CS16GS : For further information contact Gareth Stevens, New York, New York at 1-800-542-2595.

CONTENTS

Words in the glossary appear in **bold** type
the first time they are used in the text.

WHAT'S A DROUGHT?

Do the plants in your garden look dry? Just like people, plants can get thirsty. Sometimes when there's no rain for a week or so during a hot summer, lawns can look brown and may even stop growing. Just watering your garden will help your plants look healthy again.

Periods of dry weather are natural. But what happens when there's little or no rain for many months or even years? A very long dry period like this is called a drought.

Facts on Tap

You have to water your garden carefully. Just wetting the surface soil isn't enough. Make sure there's enough water to reach down to the roots of the plants.

These sunflowers look so dry because they're getting lots of sun, but not enough water!

IT'S OFFICIAL

Dry weather doesn't always mean there's a drought. A drought in one place may just be a dry spell in another. It all depends on the regular conditions of an area.

The National Weather Service (NWS) and the US Department of Agriculture watch weather and soil conditions closely for signs of very dry conditions. Some places have soil that holds water better than other places, making droughts happen less often. Depending on the conditions, these government groups may officially **declare** that a drought is happening.

Facts on Tap

The NWS keeps track of **precipitation** amounts for the entire United States.

Meteorologists at the NWS use computers to map the latest drought conditions.

NOT ENOUGH RAIN

When a place receives far less than the usual amount of rain, that's called a meteorological drought.

For example, Buffalo, New York, receives just over 40 inches (102 cm) of rain each year. If it received half of that, or 20 inches (51 cm), there would likely be drought conditions there. But in Phoenix, Arizona, there's just over 8 inches (20 cm) of rain a year. If it received 20 inches, that would be much more rain than usual!

Phoenix, Arizona

The driest place in the United States is Death Valley in California. Over the past 50 years, Death Valley has received only about 2.3 inches (5.8 cm) of rainfall each year.

9

THOSE POOR PLANTS

Another kind of drought is an agricultural drought, or a shortage of water at different points in a plant's growth. After seeds are planted, they need lots of water. If there's not enough water, plants may not begin to grow or fewer plants will grow.

Later, when fruits begin to **develop**, plants need a lot of water. If there's not enough, fewer fruits will grow. Those fruits that do develop will be smaller and may even taste different than usual.

Facts on Tap

When there's an agricultural drought, people may have to pay more for fruits, grains, and even meat because the need is greater than the supply.

Agricultural droughts happen because of too little precipitation. How well the soil holds on to moisture is also a big part of a drought like this happening.

11

DISAPPEARING RIVERS AND LAKES

When there's a long period of dry weather, lakes, rivers, and even underground water levels can drop. When this happens, it's called a hydrological drought.

Low lake and river water levels can cause problems for people using boats. Sometimes low water levels harm fish and wildlife. People who use lake and river water in their homes must find ways to live with less water. Dams that use water to create electricity may not be able to operate during times of drought.

Facts on Tap

Groundwater is the water underground that supplies wells and springs. When there's a drought, some wells run dry.

Meteorological droughts can lead to hydrological droughts. Not enough water seeps into the ground to keep groundwater levels steady. This can affect places far away from the area of dry weather!

well

lake

groundwater

13

PEOPLE PROBLEMS

Sometimes the actions of people can cause a water shortage. In an area that has had enough water over the years, an increase in the amount of water used can cause problems. This can happen if too many people begin to settle in a place that doesn't have enough water **resources**.

When the need for water is greater than the supply of water, it's called a socioeconomic drought. This can happen because a new neighborhood was built or a farmer started planting more fields.

facts on Tap

The hotels in Las Vegas, Nevada, use over 3 billion gallons of water every year. In a desert area, this can cause a big shortage of water resources.

The hotels in Las Vegas must try ways to **conserve** water to stop droughts from happening there.

THE DUST BOWL

During the 1930s, parts of Texas, Oklahoma, Kansas, Colorado, and New Mexico were hit with a long drought. While one cause was lack of rainfall, farmers had also used their land poorly.

The Great Plains area had been a large grassland. The roots of the natural grasses helped the soil stay in place and hold water. But farmers plowed too much of the land, and the soil was **exposed**. Big windstorms blew the dry soil around, and the area earned the name the "Dust Bowl."

Facts on Tap

During the Dust Bowl, thousands of acres of farmland lost all or most of their soil. Where did it all go? Huge clouds of wind-driven soil flew hundreds of miles and even reached the East Coast!

16

Colorado, 1936

The drought that contributed to the Dust Bowl lasted 8 years! Dust storms still happen today in places like Phoenix, Arizona, as this picture shows.

TOO DRY

In September 2015, just over 50 percent of the United States was facing drought conditions. Many states in the western United States, including Nevada, Washington, and Oregon, were part of the drought. But California has been in a state of drought since early 2013! This has made farming harder. It's also one of the reasons for an increase in wildfires.

As global **climate change** continues to cause Earth to get warmer, scientists say the droughts could get even worse.

facts on Tap

In a drought, people hope for snowstorms. Mountain snows melt in the springtime, filling **reservoirs** and increasing the amount of water in streams and lakes.

The dry conditions of a drought allow wildfires to spread quickly, which can harm homes and neighborhoods like this one in California.

19

HOW CAN WE HELP?

Many cities and states have laws about how water is used, such as cleaning and reusing **wastewater**. When there's a drought, even more rules may come into effect. In 2015, California passed many rules about conserving water. One changed the kind of grass that could be grown on lawns, allowing only plants able to withstand drought conditions.

Droughts can cause long-term harm to an area. Use the ideas on page 21 to help your town or state through a drought!

Conserve Water!

Turn off the water when you brush your teeth or wash your face.

Take a shower, not a bath, and shorten your time in there!

Ask your parents to fix a leaky sink, shower, or toilet.

Put water in the fridge to cool instead of letting the water run until it's cold enough.

Use a bucket to collect rainwater, and use it to water your garden.

Do you live somewhere there's a drought? You can help conserve water!

GLOSSARY

climate change: long-term change in Earth's weather, caused partly by human activities

conserve: to keep something from harm and not waste it

declare: to make known publically

develop: to grow and change

expose: to leave out in the open or not protected

meteorologist: someone who studies weather, climate, and the atmosphere

precipitation: rain, snow, sleet, or hail

reservoir: a place where something is stored

resource: a usable supply of something

wastewater: water that has been used

FOR MORE INFORMATION

Books

Langston-George, Rebecca. *A Primary Source History of the Dust Bowl*. North Mankato, MN: Capstone Press, 2015.

Meister, Cari. *Droughts*. Minneapolis, MN: Pogo Books, 2016.

Rustad, Martha E. H. *Droughts: Be Aware and Prepare*. North Mankato, MN: Capstone Press, 2015.

Websites

Drought for Kids
drought.unl.edu/DroughtforKids.aspx
Learn more about what causes droughts.

Save Our Water: Resources for Kids
saveourwater.com/what-you-can-do/kids/
How can you help in a drought? Find out here!

INDEX